Thresholds

Thresholds

Poems by

Beth Kanell

Cover design by Shay Culligan
Cover image by Beth Kanell
Author photo by Beth Kanell

ISBN: 979-8-90146-819-7

Kelsay Books
502 South 1040 East, A-119
American Fork, Utah 84003
Kelsaybooks.com

Acknowledgments

For honoring these poems with previous publication, I thank:

The Comstock Review: "Widow World"

Ginosko: "A Number Uncountable," "Niggun with a Yearling Deer"

Lit Shark: "Resilience, in Theory"

Making Space for the Light: "Solitaire"

Northwind Writing Award finalist: "Don't Tell the Grandsons"

San Diego Poetry Annual: "Rocks"

Soul-Lit: "Unrequested"

Written Tales: "Companion Animal"

Thresholds involve an exploration of transitions. Some of them I could not have handled on my own with grace, so I thank all those who pushed, pulled, and taught, especially MD and LG.

Contents

I.
RAGGED EDGES

Companion Animal

The desk, the screen, speaking aloud words strung like beads
a necklace for my throat—above my heart

letters laughing gently. The little listening dog, visitor from another
person's life, pokes her nose

under my arm, exhales insistent canine craving. My left hand dips
into
warm fur, reassuring. Right hand typing

—interruption, listen to the dog and the rain of remembering—
tea and toast set aside.

An adjacent kitchen, pale oats in a tall jar alongside three flours,
yeast patient and yearning

recipes worn and batter-splashed: her brown eyes regard me baking
bread, pie, dog biscuits

fingers adept, long practice. The math of cooking for one says
"minus":

says amputation

loosen the tourniquet every ten minutes. This body continues
(widow words too abstract)

blood, pulse, breath, reception of light and sound, placement
in a chair. Locate small comforts.

Next month the dog will leave, as planned. What I'll miss: her morning
eagerness, the world new each time she wakes

the way she dances, ears flying, confident, as if breath
never came with questions. Desk, screen, letters

an aching absence—inquiring animal baffled by the scent of
grief. Good girl. Good girl.

Not your fault, don't worry when I weep.

Solitaire

My mother used to lay out the cards in long “legs”
ringed fingers hovering over the red jack to placc on
the black queen, smoke from her cigarette coiling
above her short, dyed hair—burning the empty hours
until my father’s arrival, late of course, tired from work
and his office mistress. Some knowledge hurts too much
to hold onto.

Forty years from her death, I lay out a sheaf of poems—
scent of muffins in the air, mug of hot tea. I move
a sonnet toward some other sonnets, shuffle, consider
whether rhyme belongs with rhyme, or better to layer
blocky forms among spare narrow ones. I want to be
the jack of diamonds, one eye winking, still somehow able
to love my dad.

In the Cards

I notice her when I shuffle the deck: my mother,
her blue eye shadow deep around quiet eyes,
hands flickering as she cuts the pack
then lays the cards out in “legs” of solitaire—flash
her ring, neat little ruby, hard and sure. Fingers
swift. No stillness for these cards, except when she pauses
(long drag of smoke from a cigarette), studies.

Dealt in a hand of five, the words for my dead
rustle on the breakfast table. I deal my mother Love
(simpler when we are no longer arguing) and pass
Fascination to my father, telling him he can keep
or discard. I know him; he will discard, to prove
he’s a free agent. I never played bridge. Cards
come into focus, rearranged by suit, worn Queen
whose small freckles, like my mother’s, fit her
for family life. That expectant gaze! Creases
at the corners, still worth a discard and draw.

Escape-Now card—my cousin left the family
after he proved (in college) our dysfunction
as if analysis printed a one-way ticket. Express.
Don’t expect him back. He’s got diamonds
at his ears, clubs in his glittering nights. Unlike
that One-Eyed Jack whose slow wink emphasizes
he’s all right, all right, all right with God. Lay out
a hand and find the fifth, Scotch on the Rocks.
Sister, I’ve got a full house. Cue the music.

Don’t Tell the Grandsons

Hush: I welcome their visit at my home
which fronts the field and backs the woods, this place
where they can skip a bedtime bath, can roam
as far as courage takes them. Back-road grace!
Nor should my grown-up busy sons find out—
they need to feel I’m settled down at least.
What they can’t fix they’ll sweep aside, no doubt.
Mom must be happy now, content, at peace.

But truth is like this morning’s half-cleared skies:
one moment blue, one moment dark with rain.
Widowed, I ache for those strong arms, dark eyes
that saw and loved me well: bold joy, matched pain.

Don’t tell the grandsons. Help them light their fire
to make s’mores. Grandma is great, a careful, willing liar.

Cicada Spring

Wherever it's warmer than Vermont, cicadas that spring
scraped upward through the last hard inch of soil
forsook their nymph forms, emerge winged, red-eyed, impatient

My true love's dead; I keep aging
silver beyond his reckoning—his arms stilled, shriveled,
his coffin a safe place cicadas cannot enter

Friends in Maryland said their dog darted to cicada shells
inhaled the insect musk with passion, mouthed the husks
heaped by slender tree trunks—I remember New Jersey, seventh
grade

only the shy boys came to me. Tongue-tied
they scuffed worn sneakers on cicada shells, peered
sideways with dark eyes. I teased a bit, dared them

sliding along the slate sidewalks, silvered squares of stone
careful to avoid each crevice: cicada carapaces scattered
crunching under my feet, each a crackled testament

stung, afraid, I made a basket of my fingers, laced
across my face, as if I would not, could not see
those long lashes fluttering at the boys' eyes; their wet lips

The stones still speak their names: Katz, Fleischman, Cohen,
Levy, the likenesses my father denied, turned from, shunned
all the strange familiar that I ached for, elusive, essential

three cicada lifetimes till I found love; seventeen years of delight
then he crumbled into dark soil, his grave wide and deep
beside a blossoming tree, scarred, struggled, desired

Another cicada spring (seventeen, seventeen) behind me.
Cicadas swept from last year's grave. I shed, I crack, I cleave, I leave
my emptied shell. Against that granite marker.

Augury

Seven birds call out to the blue sky, their loud cries
echoing from the unleaved tree. I cut a long branch
to reach the swollen buds—pussywillows happening.
At the edge of the road the stream insists on singing
in patches, as snowcrust guards the field.
Something dark trembles underneath.
Let not my dead rise here. Let their pungent souls
move upward, steamy and thick, to some heaven
where the cycle ceases. Here, growth erupts with pollen
and petals; it surges forth for three seasons and then
collapses and rots, to feed the next spring. Seven blades of grass
turn green next to the house. Tracks of deer surround them.
My dead no longer feed on almonds and honey.
At Easter, the dead throw off their wrappings and walk.
They break bread, and summon, and beam proudly.
They forgive the way they died. They insist,
"Love is fragrant. In the incense, in the woodsmoke,
in the faint perfume of an apple blossom, notice me."
But let not my dead rise here today.
Yours, my friend, yours are coming closer.
I hear them rustling in the nearby woods. Seven
ladybugs crawl up the window. Seven peepfrogs call;
seven distant eagles soar. Seven wishes.
I send them to you: that your dead may rise
today.

Unanswered

By ten at night the widow's house is tired and whispering
—oh yes, it's been a long day—no reply

and this bed, ready for another night half filled,
balances on three feet, swinging the fourth as if

wounded. In the kitchen the kettle whistles like a train
oh it's hard to face a god at ten at night.

Not a desert deity in white sheets; no keffiyah, no agal
(that circlet of rope), no ram's horn sounding from the ridge

Not a smoking torch setting fire to the branches
piled around the limbs of childhood; no lamb in the thorns

Not the unfamiliar words of a sabbath prayer on paper
or this struggling tongue or half-remembered tune

There are angels of bereavement
of exhaustion

They carry swords; they bring a smoky scent with them
Once two young lovers shared a garden

Now I grip the bars of the iron gate, about to climb it anyway
wrestle with a messenger of better intentions

There was a tree of life; death dangles from the other tree,
draped—

I shared a promise; I made a vow; I can only pursue

This Other who seizes; who blazes; who cries out
across this barren field.

Wilderness

It's another green and blue spring, with sunshine spilling
over the eager gardens, and trees spreading leafy fingers, so
it looks like it should be easy—all of the customers

at the boots-and-pocket-knives store have stopped wearing masks
and so has the owner. You can see their photo in the paper
which is delivered in the wee hours of star and moon time

by someone in a modern Jeep, who spreads the news among
all of us. How the schools have struggled; how the stores,
open now after years of pandemic, hang welcome signs

and how the food banks multiply, counting the hungry, who
now are called food-insecure. If you prefer, count the cars
that bustle along this back road, which accepts the traffic

of people turning aside, looking for a greener route. We have
finished wiping down doorknobs and purchases; finished
worrying about who'll catch the virus next; daily,

another service scheduled that once was postponed.
In the wilderness, carry a shovel and a rock bar; prepare to sing
your loneliness. If you hold it inside, like a tiny fleck of

nonliving DNA, it may attach to a cell and multiply. You can't
afford that kind of despair. Call someone. Bake another loaf
of bread. The little market in town? Butter's on sale there,

because the dairy farms can't stop milking. You need more,
to spread on warm slices that carry comfort, along with a story of
how hard they had it in the old days. There could be worse

wilderness to walk, you know; others have had it hard too, and
they didn't have such good boots to wear. The little things.
Let's count them now, together.

A Number Uncountable

Anniversaries crop up in poets' work so often,
fingering a calendar date that drips with loss or
glows in retrospect. My neighbors who go to Florida
post with joy at the "gotcha" date of their rescue dog,
while I walk toward death.

Widow world is time-stamped, and the fortunate
have a bit of warning—weeks, months, even years
to see the end of shared nights and diner breakfasts
for two. Click another year into place, continue
saying goodbye. Which never

ends. Today I also watch the endless count of bigger
losses, like the man whose brother died of gunshot
(whose finger on the trigger?), the grandchildren of
the last lynching someplace else, baby destined for
death in the first breath. But

I have never tried to count the years since my ex spouse
threaded darkness with his .45 next to him, seeking me
(his girlfriend called to warn "go someplace else"), or to sift
those hundreds of nightmares twisted by my father's
insistence on new lovers.

No, if I'm going to spend time counting the uncountable
give me a moonless night of stars so dense, so constantly
yearning, that numbers fall apart: Big Dipper, Little Dipper,
long-lived monsters and heroes journeying the widest
arc of impossible distance.

Lying on my back, feeling the pulse of the iron-hearted earth,
sharing the air inhaled by passing porcupines and deer,
I'd teach my city grandsons to wish on that swift meteor—
my own life shrinking to night's lush aromas, wrapped with
something uncountable.

Are You Dating Yet?

It’s not like buying some new car, I didn’t tell him,
sighing over product reviews, maker news, ratings
in lines of stars. Not a replacement of worn parts
or pumping helium into the heart. Who needs
a floating, flying heart? Or some sagging red balloon
that farts when you untie the knot? Grief clots.
I didn’t say wait till you’ve heard the cry
when Death settles, the musty stink of his dark suit,
worn and torn, sworn in spit and tears. Salted,
sanctified, blunt as a casket: not some
flimsy basket of regrets, but muscled, weighty,
freighted and freckled with not-yets. I could pretend
I didn’t hear him. Simple, shorter than giving warning—
“too serious, too mysterious,” don’t ask again:
Widow world has its rough rules, rusted grief,
Death hunched like a tough thief on parole, eyes cold
bribing the night with fool’s gold, so I told him
I’m not looking—lucky enough to have once found
one wild soul to make me whole. No backhand roll
of love’s dice; once, twice, then tossed them right.
I bit my tongue when he asked, tonight: didn’t tell him
he’s sure to learn how it feels. The question’s surreal.
What does he have that Death will itch to steal?

Viral

I knew it would get a lot of Likes: the photo of the young man
lifting his dog as if she were a woman who'd given up legs
for the sake of love, just like that mermaid, who gave her tail.
Labels stick. The feed applies them. Dog, man, tree. This is

a photo of love the easy way. Last week I caught (with my lens)
tipped faces of farmers listening to each other, holding words
for each other, to consider after germination. Even so, I knew
it wasn't going to get a lot of hearts, or smileys—ordinary

hardly ever goes viral. Dogs, though, that's something else. I saw
this white furball with a jeweled collar, posing on a kitchen chair
in someone else's photograph. Hard to believe how many shares
it gained by afternoon—hope, darling, precious, sweet,

all the words I didn't hear when I was growing up (oldest child,
make sure the others eat their supper, clean their rooms), hushed
and reminded: Be seen, not heard. Be good in school. Be clean,
learn words. Study more, perform on tests, be best. Grateful now

that I wasn't looking for angel wings or commentary—I'd have laid
my soul at an altar if something holy asked me to, and parents
(mine) were halfway there, rod and staff, pointing toward
that thicket where a scapegoat struggled. A goat will not go viral, either,

unless it's just a kid. One time, I did.

Thrift-Shop Punctuation Marks

My mittens, worn thin, were cut from two wool sweaters
purchased, used, when my boys were small; now
they're tall men, who text to check that Mom is walking,
talking, unbroken. So far, so good, I say, as I bend
with the day. Grip a railing. Watch the ice.

Let's say the mittens, placed on the table, could be
parentheses: between the curve of the left hand
and the right hand's thumb, insert a sentence,
paragraph, chapter. Lay out the wide fabric of love
then the gash of loss, the hanging threads.

Dreams of my beloved. Which was his favorite shirt? Where
did I donate his warm sweaters? Who exulted, bought
that pack of extra-large socks, unopened, never worn,
the ones I took to the thrift shop after his death?

Inscribe this between my aging mittens: Letting go is
never done. His lips, stilled and cooling; his cheek,
kissed so often it should be called "used"; fingers
curved to meet my own. I tell my boys I'm fine.
No sense saying I'm putting on my mittens.

Rope Burn

At two this morning the phone began to ding
agitated texts from a confused son—
easy for him to press “send” and for me to wake,
my stomach roiling, fumbling for the light.

“You have to let them go.” Everyone tells you
except for the times when they remind you:
“Keep your family close together.” What strings
do we use? What bonds? Slip knots?

Leafing through old letters: My mother asked
(time and again) how I was doing, what I liked,
what she should send for my birthday,
surely I felt roped into her daily need to love

and to care about and care for. These strands:
balloon silk is one thing, but the ropes that bind
the basket are another. Callouses thicken on my palms
a raw burn across the pad of my thumb.

Only let go. Only hold close. At two in the morning
only keep plenty of gas in the car. And a flashlight.

Oh Wicked Winds

It's March kicking the edge of April, spitting
pellets of old snow from a moody sky
when yesterday I thought winter was quitting.

This morning started almost warm; I even tried sitting
on the steps, struck by sudden sun, eyes dry,
skin flushed, eager. All winter, I've been gritting

my teeth, clenched fists, fighting it, fitting
loss into variations on a long goodbye—
then this gray afternoon, grief's grip abruptly quitting.

Not that I'll forget it—just that the pain is sitting
where childbirth's pains did, real but pushed aside by
a red insistence of breath, blood, life itself fitting

into unexpected north winds. No more knitting
self-pity or desolation or a woeful "why"
but shouting back to that swift storm, splitting

a toothed and hungry passion, instead of quitting!
Yesterday's brown grief was a garment fitting
while I suffered and let death make me cry—
now wicked winds swirl, raw and raucous: spitting!

On the Street

Wealth builds across generations. This, I've read,
is a long-term cost of American slavery: grandparents
unable to give a down payment.

How simple it might sound, to fall in love.

My son got married in Korea. Red envelopes
in a basket at the reception: money for the future.
Thousands of dollars—no, thousands of *won.*
I have not set enough aside. My envelope: thin.

Dried fruits, nuts, symbolic in Buddhist vows.

Some people braid their differences into strong ropes.
I've found the bitter remains caught in back teeth,
unswallowed, coarse. Divorce. Prenup?

Near my home, New England graveyards bright with markers:
Families paid in blood.

White houses, brick storefronts, churches with steeples
and a soup kitchen near the laundry. Statistics: more than thirty
homeless teens this winter. In one small town. My son has starved
on couches, slept on roofs, phoned to say "I'm cold, Mom."

On the corner, not far from the high school, a man with red
cheeks, hand-lettered sign. HUNGRY. Though I empty my pocket
and tell him the cheapest diner in town, I'm helpless for tomorrow.

That man's too old to have a mother waiting, by the phone.

Wealth builds across generations. Poverty smells like an open
drain;
hot showers are a luxury, while clothing at the laundromat
gets stolen. I might go back to that corner: hand him woolen socks.

Winter strips us to food and shelter. Can love build up
without those generations? Don't weep in winter, your nose will
run.
Red envelope. Red frost-scarred cheeks. Regret.

Widow World

It's the Uncertainty Principle brought to life: Nobody checks
whether I am alive and breathing, or dead of heat stroke
in the endlessly needy garden, where weeding has replaced
walking last spring's resident dog. Each morning I post photos
(secret gateways between thick trees, openings to fields where
last night's deer strolled, their eyes wide enough to capture
stray rays of moon and star; velvety petals of deep-red lilies
and the purple fringes of vetch, those field's-edge survivors)
so I figure two or three days of no new photos online and friends
would begin to send me "just checking" messages. Meanwhile,
I talk aloud to the unspeaking ghost of the man who needed
all my love, all my listening, steady bass-line of my former life—
Notice, I tell myself now, that you can confirm your sanity
from this silence. This unanswered tenderness. This empty
chamber of the ear, which hosts the hum of the refrigerator
without naming it. Hours of liminal, of a pause button with
a tiny blue light to signal that recording is "off" until an email
lands, clunky and off balance, in the computer's lap, or the buzz
and tremble of the phone signals a passing car, alerting
security cameras. Is the cat inside the box or outside? You
can't tell till you open the flap. Observing is a blade,
sharp and shiny, thumbed into position at the box-cutter's tip
a little gummed by many strips of tape. The Zoom camera
forces the computer's eye to blink, lid lifting, electric,
neither wave nor particle but surveillant, panopticon; do you
trust that the camera is off when the light stops? Maybe God,
an absent-minded ally almost awake, notices how dull breakfast
was; how a little work to be done seeps and puddles, waiting for
attention; how a voice alone whispers and echoes in ordinary
not-quite-quiet silence; how I breathe, sniff, slap where
a mosquito's tracked the scent of warm skin. Wake up, I say to
the Sorry Self sinking into the chair. Go, go forth, feet, socks,
boots. Don't be the cat fainting inside that taped, unmoving box.

Geese

Autumn colors ride the hills, and the air snaps cold, then teases
back to something easier. Each morning I hear the geese

organizing each other toward the corn field up the ridge.
Each evening they return to the lake in the valley, sometimes

low over the house so I can see their wide chests, rounded bellies,
necks outstretched for those persistent calls. I remember

how I listened for his voice down the hallway, my name spoken
or shouted, depending on whether it was a moment to laugh
together

(bending over the pages to see what he'd discovered) or, more
often toward the end, a plea for help: To stand together. To walk.

Check it on the Internet: Geese mate for life, spend their days
touching each other, calling each other, winging together

toward the day's grazing, the night's safety in the waters. I fear
for each goose now: aware that grief and mourning swell

in the throat, cause the heart to clench, force a new call
of loneliness as thick as the gray October clouds. Let each

live, unmolested by fox or hunter, I pray. Let the pairing be
safe. Let the calls over the hills be excitement and plans,

mapping their departure for southern golf courses, estuaries,
wide blue lakes. Let them see retirement. I have no urge

to walk away from my sorrow. It wears a face, and the face
is the one that, goose-hearted, I call out to see, touch,

slide a hand down the new-shaven cheek. No regrets.
These gray hairs becoming abundant? Feathers.

Crossing

There are two reasons to cross over:
because you crave the other side, or you crashed,
clear out of choices. Water, let me walk.

No sense summoning river fog or the lake's
late mist, drifting, silver, shivering. Only listen, as
loons salute before sunrise. Water, weep.

Which way: stepping stones, a borrowed boat,
a bridge of bones? Bold until broken. I ache to arch
arms forward, swimming. Crawl. Kick.

Water, whisper: Does this bridge boast rails?
Seal the winter pond, let the ice thicken, willing, white,
warning. The brush of boots. Swish and slip.

Grasp one end of a tree-tied rope, tug
against its terminal; wrestle and wrap, pull tight, fight
forward. Migrating dove's inner magnet,

bubble within the buried turtle, chill pink glow
edging the last dark hour before dawn. Sole star, Venus,
dim and departing, dropping down. When you

choose to cross to that shore, call.
If I can, I'll come. Seek, sing, summon.
Water, where I've willingly waded.

Crossing now. Come across.

Unrequested

When your child gets a diagnosis instead of a cure
you enter the wilderness: sun-baked sand, dry wind.

Your father dies. Everyone knew he was that sick
and they called you home, to an edge of the wilderness.

Some people know how to pack: a soft leather case
holds fabric to drape an altar, a cup, a spoon. They know

north from the Big Dipper. Which of the seeping waters
can be consumed. Which ones, only to wash with. Words

to pin onto the haunting melody, a descant
that harmonizes with grief. Find a dry gourd, hollow it

carve out a space to blow into; song from a dry throat,
while you dream of yesterday's deep and stone-lined well—

The risen moon, sharpening every shadow, hums
like someone else's mother at bedtime, tucking the covers.

Your map is unreliable. Stars forget to speak your language.
When an old woman gazes into your face, then your palm,

she tells you: Expect wilderness. Raw, burnt, exhausted,
whether your tears wet your cheeks or are swallowed.

Wise ones walk the wilderness with sturdy shoes,
sunscreen, a few friends. Wear white. Can rest without pillows

when the body begs. Before this, you dreamed of disaster;
now, damp with evening dew, imagine the scent of angels.

Niggun with a Yearling Deer

> *Niggun*: "wordless song . . . a means of elevating the soul to God."
> —Encyclopedia Brittanica, online

Hush, sss, hush, shh, the ears flick
they twitch, quick, the small hooves that snap a stick
in front of us a yearling deer: it holds
the stillness of the nearby trees without a breath or breeze
will freeze in place but through a gap
of branches there's the wide-eyed face:

yai-la-lai, those big dark eyes and
lai-lai-dai the mother deer, the doe, replies,
a sniff, a snort, a huff of air:
this too is breath of the creation
scented with the damp rich earth
la-lai, la-lai, the yearling's small new fascination—

doe licks her offspring; I've kissed mine.
Grandchild at my side, eyes wide, discovering
(la-dai, la-dai) that each small sound among the trees

reveals another bird or beast. I touch his hand
and point with care, the yearling deer is standing
there, we start to step, we try, we dare
but those long ears are well aware

and with a leap and crash of brush
it takes the risk, it breaks the hush
an urge to flee, to leap, to rush:

hush, sss, hush, shh, grandchild tiptoes at my side
a bluejay cries, and butterflies
rise up along the path we take.

Yai-lai-la-lai, we focus fiercely
hushed and hoping for the sound
the yearling deer may make
when it lies down.

Resilience, in Theory

"natural areas provide restorative qualities, help with
physiological and psychological aspects of coping
after a disaster"

oh my babes

foreseen predicted inevitable
still my home's broken open, heart wounded, head

a scalp wound, they say, bleeds fiercely

this death

yet how can I deny the solace
of walking the back road, the mallard paddling
in the pond on the ridge

while its mate hides, considers a nest
though these small waters won't hold them long

you were my shelter

now rainy days are gentler than
sunshine

spattering the leaves

restoration, like rehabilitation,
at dusk

II.
SUSPENSE

First Day of Radiation

Someone said "imagine the rays as golden sun,
soaking into you, bringing healing." I, in my science mind,
know they are death rays. The task is direct: Kill those
rebels, those misfired cells that tried to multiply
when they were only supposed to soak quietly
in the salty brine of the body's warmth. Track them,
eliminate them, burst them and let the marvelous system
sweep up all the broken bits and send them out. Kidney
efforts, I know. Drink more water.

Science mind is good. Death rays have a task,
and I can collaborate and keep moving. To my littlest
brother, though (the one who's taller than me, stronger,
only a decade younger but forever a kid to this big
sister who helped him toddle), I confess: I glow green
at night now. My x-ray vision is developing. Look out,
by the middle of next week I'll see inside your pockets!
He answers: Glowing green, great, much safer for your
twilight, dawnlight, walks.

Preparation

I anoint my breast with oil:
that is, with cream of aloe and vitamins,
preparing for the flame. That is,
the high-tech beam of radiation
focused and precise, aimed between four
tattoo'd dots on my skin. This is no
exaggeration: ink pressed through needle
permanent compass marks on my chest.
Which is to say, the small voice that
whispers after the earthquake, after
storms, after hidden hour sobbing
with terror of death, yes, that voice
instructs the cells in motion, as if
they were stars in miniature. These
constellations of nucleus, breath, pulse
compound and dance behind the nipple
cupped now by the surgeon's arc. Scar.
Roseate reminder of what was, is,
will be. On Tuesday, the fire.
I anoint my breast with oil.

Andromeda

The steel table is narrow, high, complicated, adjustable.
It's covered with a sheet. I perch on it, swing my legs up
onto the clever support for knees, untie the gown
and lie back, head tilted sideways. There's a head holder.
Tugging short fabric strips the younger women twist my torso.
I'm naked like a statue—reaching my arms overhead, gripping
two wooden poles, strong. All this arranging opens
my breast, my underarm, these newly scarred "lady parts"
to the waiting machine. With nymph voices, soft, coaxing,
the "techs" measure, adjust, make ready the energy beam.
I am a glowing galaxy, and the x-rays are shooting stars,
arcing through my gravitation.

Each time they lay me out, I shut my eyes, pray as the beast
growls. On a screen behind their concrete shield
the techs watch my ribs rise and fall— "when you're ready,
take a breath and hold it"—they aim radiation, focus, pierce
tight muscles and dark caverns where rogue cells hide.
Breast cancer. The beast, the techs, and I in my nakedness
dance. We prance a cliff above ocean waves, test tides,
place wagers for survival. Death to the tumor cells;
rebirth to the healthy. Nymphs press buttons. Rays
slice through skin, burning as they pass the nipple,
swift, sharp, precise. Beyond my closed eyes a red light
glows, blazes, insists; violet after-shadows haunt
my nerves. Teeth clenched, breath insistent in narrowed
nostrils: suddenly my dead mother's face overlays mine
as the sharp scent of my underarms discloses terror.
They never really leave, do they, our dead?

Beyond the rational, the precise, the medical, I meet
untamed creation. In its grasp, I am nebula spun,
galaxy spilled, star upon star in ancient patterns
named for mythic power. Here, the king, Cepheus. There,
crown of his wife, Cassiopeia. Perseus and his battle cry
destined to behead monsters, earn a princess:
Andromeda. Translate to mean, "She who had no choice."
Chained to a rock to appease the ocean's rage; torn free
to marry; too female (those breasts) to assert separation
from menace, monster, threat of death.

This will not last forever. Today, an hour.
More women cross paths in the waiting room,
arrange head scarves and wigs or (half-ashamed of luck)
finger what hair remains. We choose this.
We pack for it, train for it, map its constellations
in harsh hours after diagnosis.

Two days later I lie again on the narrow table, eyes closed
breath slowed. The careful tech aligns my bones
assures me all is ready—silently slips a band around my feet
to hold my position. I am Andromeda
perched, eagle-eyed. I am a sacrifice
who embraces the fire—one who aims her breath
encourages and invites flame. Red light flares.
I exhale with care, hum harmony to the machine:
song of power, shattering yesterday's manacles. Words rise,
a moon-tide of assurance. Arched back, upthrust pelvis.
Open passage. Monstrous birth.

Tell Me

Tell me about the forty years: how those lost, lost people
trudged through sandstorms and disaster, carrying tents,
arguing over which tribe had more honor.
How foolish it must have seemed to the women in labor
straining to release babies from safety into risk. And for
those preparing the meals, hundreds to feed and often
only "manna": manna fried, manna scrambled,
manna crisp and morning fresh with clear water
not yet steamed by the blazing sun.

I have forty days of radiation: that fierce number,
neither the forty days of rain on the animal-overloaded ark
nor the forty days of thirst and hunger before Jesus believed
he'd prepared himself. Find the way. We who scrub
the inside-out fabrics of our garments and bedding, pounding
the stains against rocks, grateful for water to rinse them,
laying the fabrics flat in the sun to dry, we know. There's gratitude,
for days when the rain holds off until sundown. Which wilderness
is this one? Theirs, his, mine? Or the Wilderland, darkened.

The mountains here seem neat and trim from a distance.
I think, "I could climb that, and find my way." Then,
under the trees, and circling the cedar tangles and the swampy
stretches and climbing a massive tumble of rocks,
my shadow appears in front of me—when I know that the angle
of the sun, and my chosen direction, should angle my shadow
like a pointer behind my left shoulder. I named these
"hill," and "ridge," and "height of the land." When did they
become "mountain of confusion"? When did they turn,

in the green ferocity of May rains, into
pathless forest of other direction? I need to be home
in forty minutes. Work is waiting for me.

My father's voice, mumbled around his pipe stem:
Water runs downhill. Follow it, my girl.

Deliver to the Breast Cancer Team, Please

Dear radiation therapists ("When you're ready")
the burned skin is sloughing off: white leaves
of farewell, detaching like the end of love
which can be, is, as tender as its beginning.
My second husband died at forty, his body
on the hospital bed while the machines kept his heart
warm and active, waiting for transport to a city
where his organs, even the lenses of his blue eyes
became a treasured harvest. His last wife—
I was the one from the middle years—stood guard
at the door, determined soldier facing her loss.
The sons arrived to say goodbye. And I,
who loved him so long ago, but loved with all my
heart, bent to touch the dark curl by his ear
my fingers remembering passion and kisses
("take a deep breath") hunger and exhilaration
how we loved! Years ago now, but in that moment
my hands reminded all of me: this body, ah,
this person. This love. He said my woman breasts
seemed large, ample, lovely. As the scorched skin peels
and I stroke more salve over the ragged surface
this is the "kiss it better" moment. Love lasts,
beyond the radiation's fierce efforts. Worth another
marriage, and a happy one now. Still I miss your
voices, ladies, steady and reliable, my eyes closed
to the machine's red glow. Thanks for the hope and magic.
("And hold it.")

In This Day

Everything is all right
No it's not, I'm behind on work, have been since the last
day of radiation, struggling to bring in enough to make up for those

But everything is all right
There's a new bird at the bird feeder, small with tiny feathers
that puff out for warmth on this chilly autumn day

And everything is all right
But I ran out of money last spring—still, scraped up enough
for the roofers to be here this fall, hammering over my head
which somehow isn't thinking as quickly as a year ago

Maybe that's just what it is to grow older, a little slower
a few more mistakes here and there but

it's all right, really, a few mistakes never killed anyone
at least not while typing, not even while cooking
(did I really spread mint icing on the apple donuts? ick)

yes everything is all right
Balance is the key: taking time to write a poem
means you'll be forty dollars short from work
because there is no free lunch, no paid leave, no way
to make up for how things change but

it's sure to be all right, just a little further, a little more
labor—air out the room, let it be a day to start over
sunlight and a glimpse of blue sky over the trees

where it's all right, it's all right, the apples will
come again next year; this was an "off year" which happens
just like the little lemon seed nodule, the apple seed tumor
the nuclear electronic mathematic radiation wrapped up
within the calm muscles of the massive machine

which obeys each typed command of those capable women
measuring treatment, burning away problems, making a
clear space for something healthy to return

oh yes, everything is all right
it's the six-month checkup, meeting again the smiles, kindness

Ask me about it: Everything is (it really is) all right.

III.
MAPS

Surveyor's Manual

Loose, faulty, and ignorant conveyances—
that is, the documents describing the land that's sold
or inherited
What would you do today if there were no tomorrow
heavy demands upon the surveyor
concerning boundaries and landmarks
Why are you asking, is the cancer awake again
having children means one constant direction
magnetic north
Find the spot where the line truly exists
—death can't be undone—
the work and training of the surveyor
stability of property and peace of community
Who built that fence, wrong line, wrong post
Katie you are always in my prayers
the spot where the line truly
What is the point of accurately measuring
uncertain things
fear of failure shadowing the surveyor day by day
So much more than wearing an orange vest, hi-vis jacket
destined to wrestle with problems of the line
this very distinct need
"The watchwords of the surveyor are
Patience and Common Sense"
isolated in his calling
across the desert of dry details
a course pointed out by probability
and landmarks:
notched trees, iron pipes—
How should you oil your boots, before heading out?

Pre-Surgery Outline

Like empathy, children have to learn how a map,
even one of just their row of houses, corresponds with
what they see: the little labeled boxes, the street,
short line standing for a ten-minute walk.

Once on a boat I watched blue scribbles on a screen—
"That's my fishfinder," someone said—I only saw wiggling
lines and constant change. Last spring, after the MRI,
gazing at mysterious gray speckled images

I hoped the doctors knew them like a fishfinder
or the green map on my phone's bright screen, where
a two-finger caress brings up the names of the roads
and I can find myself, know where I am.

Wouldn't it be nice to see blue lines across my belly
the dotted ones labeled "cut here, one inch depth,"
safety reminders about buried power lines and water?
Map me, I tell the surgeon as I drift toward

anesthesia's misty landscape. Scalpel, clamp, eyepiece:
Here are my rivers and my empathy. Follow and find.

Lost in Translation

The mapped fragments of yesterday's genes
go "whoops" as they skip and replicate
and poof! just like that, something's lost—

me, I lost two marriages to divorce
and the third, as expected, to death;

cars of course (what happened to that VW?)
my mother, unwilling to pass in mid life

night hours spent reading too late, predicting
a next-day nap would fill the gap (it didn't)

snails found the zinnias, leaves pierced like colanders
giving way to wild geraniums after hard rain
blowsy and purple-petaled

discovered an old brick among the late iris
and last week, that button to my winter coat
lost again today

See the DNA strands dance, dosey-doh
swing your partner, grand right and left while
a snipper molecule zips along the route, trimming

so the baby's nose won't look out of place
Mrs. W's children all have that white streak of hair

one night I lost my technical virginity
later I swear the lifeline on my palm wilted

How do you translate meant-to-be into
mountain mist and wind-tossed rain?
I think I found an app for that

watching the compass needle tremble
how do you say
the river finds the fish.

Star Chart

A neighbor nudged me to watch for northern lights
on Friday night. But clouds rolled in, thick curtains
humid, not yet raining. I looked north anyway, pinned
with the long ache of absence. Clenched.

Maybe I had a past life (before him) of shepherd, years
and years, centuries ago, lying on my folded cloak
under some sort of mythic oak, the fragrant breath of sleep
rising from nearby sheep—and in the sky above,

an arc of stars in the same fashion these clouds hide, sparks
named for bears and dragons, power of widowed passion—
Meant-to-Be, Found-at-Last, pantheon in a distance
dimmed by death. Mark and measure in memory:

his arm flung across to me in his sleep. Star map,
queen always reaching for king, hunter for hound,
my lips for his bristled cheek. While I wait, watching,
a slow glow edges the dark. Northern lights persist,

beyond my cloud-wrapped blindness. I constellate
his kindness.

Unmapping

Sometimes I balance a fork on a finger: testing the weight
finding a pivot point a little closer to one end. Real,
though approximate. What shaped my life was my father, the scent
of his vanilla-laden tobacco, that British sarcasm and
his grudging praise for me: "not bad."

My secret lover in the north, slowly licking my bare
shoulder, could heat even a winter cabin with the flames
he'd ignite in me. Before I understood, he whispered
"Sometimes your father seems to be in the room
with us." Lifted eyebrow. Flicking tongue.

Sometimes luck drives the right side of the road, opens
a locked door, flips the map, hacks the GPS. Other than gonads
no match of my soulmate to my father. None.
Zilch. In the board game "Sorry!" there's a safety zone—
mine, head on his chest, our hands linked.

So my unmapping came at last, with that tender, kind man:
how he knew (before I guessed) I was the one for him, reached
for me; how even the parts of me that baffled him, like
hot flashes and poetry, he trusted. Death collected him
early, but he'd redrawn my lines.

Five years after the burial, one morning I shuddered awake
in dry sobs: "You're not coming back, are you?" Knew
empty unmapped space. Felt the press of grown sons,
offering to redefine me as an old woman fading, frail: No.
Burst through the door. Triangulate the trails.

Controlled Conditions

In high school biology I grabbed the idea: how the investigator
sets up a controlled condition, which is normal, unchanged,
unaltered in the experiment. Like what you get by starting a seed
in a pot of ordinary soil, with ordinary watering.
Say, a pea. Say, twice a week, eight ounces.

And then, in a second pot, you put the second pea in more soil
(from the same batch—control what you can) and water it
on the same days as its sister. But with an ounce of Mom's vodka
measured into the water each time. Assess at the end of
two weeks. Did the second plant grow taller?

The first one was your control. I picture the second pea
thriving at first on extra minerals, racing toward two inches
way ahead of the first potted pea. Let the experiment last
long enough, though. See the cost. What we should have realized
would kill her sooner or later. *Sooner.*

Not an alcoholic's liver but an exploding heart. How surprised
she'd be to have faded, to yield. So I carry her each morning,
    walking
up the ridge, picking out flowers she named, the arch of an apple-
laden branch, bringing home a nice stone for the rock garden.
Still, change continues:

Facing surgery, routine but scary anyway, agreeing to allow
six slices into my belly and a month of recovery, I walked toward
a planned invasion eating a diet designed to prepare my organs
for the clever doctor: I followed the intervention she prescribed,
pre-op diet meant to tame (she said)

my liver. Insist on change. No control.

Earthworm DNA

Crickets click the sequence into the summer air:
a-t-g-c-g-a-t-g-a, with a final t,
though only the other crickets really hear
meaning. This is the earthworm chromosome
beginning to wriggle. When I was a child
grieving for the accident of slicing (with my shovel)
that shining mysterious creature into two,
my mother reassured me: each half, she said,
will grow again. Like the starfish, which can grow
a new body—two stomachs in each, and both
ovaries and testicles—from each severed arm.

Everything my mother told me about sex: wrong.
Love doesn't fix it, and it doesn't fix love. Worms
can't regenerate from both halves, only from
the mouth end—which is called the head
although there are no eyes. Five hearts per
earthworm but no lungs. Tomorrow I can walk
through a waterfall and taste awe; at dusk, track DNA
in the cricket song; in the night, seek the missing
part of my life, the other half of my heart
given willingly to the kindest of men. I cannot
regenerate what's been cut away by death,

though I examine the genome of worms, t-c-t-a-c,
wondering what's been lost in translation. Mapping
possibilities for the return of nerves. Long timeline.
Love is not a bodily function, and my mother
had her reasons to mistrust it. Half my genes
are hers. Bone cells regenerate in a year, nerves
(if not severed) in months. Earthworms? Each
regenerates garden soil, g-g-t-c grieving.

Genetic Mapping

The teen from Japan, applying for a license,
asked me the color of his eyes. "What does your
passport say?" "Nothing," he pointed out. "In Japan
we all have the same eyes."

Later, I stared into the mirror, dodging a bit
to catch the clearest parts (old mirrors have funky
patches from aging). Hazel, my mother taught me.
Green, with brown and hints of—

Is this one gene's determination? Two? His and hers
twined together in a chromosome, mirror of one
person's pleasure, another's willingness. It makes me
sad now, so much my mother yielded.

Science displays genes as mapped and coded.
"Green is recessive to brown" the map key proves,
"but dominant to blue," and if that makes a palette of
family, mine's maybe a melanin mess.

Stubbornness is dominant (mark it X), although
wanting to move farther is recessive to the bank account,
so the only time I saw Japan myself was in an airport
on the way to a wedding in Korea.

Most DNA results arrive in an email now and tell you
whether you like cilantro. The nerves in noses determine
who you'll find irresistible. Who you'll ache to touch,
tongue, swallow; who you'll never forget.

In summer, along the edges of back roads (this place
I live, where my mother might have thrived) yellow flowers
called buttercups reflect sunny moments. Mom used to say
"hold it under your chin, do you like butter?"

I like it melted into a baked potato. Otherwise it's like cilantro
(soapy in my mouth). Epigenetics claims experience alters
genes. Like the map that opens on the phone: searching
for roads not taken, using two fingers.

Hesitation

After a month of flooding, who would dare to stand
beside the river's gully, perch, balance over riven ground
rise to a ballerina's pointe and extend her arms:

I find few reassurances beside these swollen waters,
froth of mountain spit riding the rush, rocks dividing current
then the sharp crack of lightning overhead.

Yet here I stand—poised to abandon wakefulness and words,
prepared to yield my will to anesthesia's warm hands,
meeting the surgery's demands. Breath and heartbeat

dependent on a small man in blue cotton, masked, with
three machines whose green lines flare and tremble
echoing this resistant, resilient pulse.

Months of intelligent conversation and medical language
convinced me there is no other sensible choice—incision,
soft exhalation, blood vessels bitten in toothed clamps

then the strangers' hands moving within the bounds of body
leveraging my miscreant organs into apposite archipelago in salted
streams. Let the anesthetic overpower my resistance

let my fierce independence dip, drowse, demand nothing
except the oversweet sleep of the drugs dripping down darkness
and then—ah, what dreams may come? Could I host

a honeyed presence of tenderness and heart's ease? Or will
my life's unsilenced questions rise up, desperate to wake me,
shorn of reply, taunted by those sharp bold blades?

Hesitant at this slick edge, tossing flowers into the waters,
one last long weekend before the plastic bracelet rings my wrist:
"The heartache and the thousand natural shocks," a whisper

of Hamlet in Ophelia's shell-like ear. There's a girl who knew
relentless rivers.

Rocks

In New England, we grow them—harvest them, stack them
along the edges of fields. Good crop? Not bad this time.
After spring's lines of lavender and late roses

half a year of long lament, laid as a line of stones. My life in
widow world: Would he have watched this season's harvest?
Praised fat tomatoes in a bowl, purple berries, pinecones?

He would. So I carry him close, as his spirit snuggles
in my hip pocket, speak his name, sing louder, share a smile.
When night falls, I shoulder silence, dinner for one:

which drove me to delve and define "inselberg,"
tongue-tossed by a mining geologist in east Africa seduced
by the Serengeti, where lions hunt from high crags—

rock knobs risen through weather and resistance. On my
tongue next, the term "monadnock," indigenous form for lone
mountain surviving. In New England we live with our past:

words absorbed from Abenaki assertion, stones heaped as walls
around our burial grounds. We witness forests reclaim farms.
Find old foundations of granite and grit

dark, cold, exhaling radon remnants. I gave my love
a marble marker for his grave, engraved with names. Geology
rasps rough on this rainy evening, looking up

igneous, formed from fire, blazing birth of coarse-grained rock
laid down in wide intrusions at this world's skin. I grasp:
granite grows a wrap of lichens, palest green, rooting

in the grains from which the stone steals its name. Words wrestle,
weathered stones subsiding into soil. Widow world wanders,
walking steep slopes; in loss, the gray-green lichens linger.

About the Author

Beth Kanell lives in northeastern Vermont among rivers, rocks, and a lot of writers. Her poems seek comfortable seats in small well-lit places, including *Lilith Magazine, The Comstock Review, Indianapolis Review, Gyroscope Review, The Post-Grad Journal, Does It Have Pockets?, Anti-Heroin Chic, Ritualwell, Persimmon Tree, Northwind Treasury, RockPaperPoem, Ginosko,* and *Rise Up Review*. She also writes feature articles, short stories, reviews, and novels, most recently *The Bitter and the Sweet.*

Join her for conversation at:
bethkanell.blogspot.com

www.ingramcontent.com/pod-product-compliance
Lightning Source LLC
LaVergne TN
LVHW020658100826
845148LV00012B/2559

* 9 7 9 8 9 0 1 4 6 8 1 9 7 *